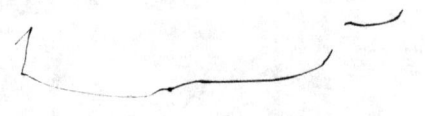

PEACE WITHIN

YOUR PEACEFUL INNER CORE

Also by Kebba Buckley Button

Discover The Secret Energized You, Book and eBook
Receptive and Ready Audiobook/Meditation CD
Embracing the Divine, Guidebook
Desert Summer Thriving, Guidebook

WISK – 2012

PEACE WITHIN

YOUR PEACEFUL INNER CORE

For Barbara,
For the Highest and Best always –
Kebba Buckley Button

Kebba Buckley Button, M.S., O.M.
The LifeTools Lady [sm]

LifeTools Press ■ UpBeat Living Media

Notice

This book is intended to be used as a general guide and source of inspiration, and is not a substitute for professional help, nor is the information intended to treat, diagnose, or cure any disorder of any type. Anyone who believes that they need more than this book provides should seek the services of a professional.

All scientific and technical information is as accurate as the author can make it within this brief work. However, since science reveals new facts every day, the author cannot guarantee that the science discussion in this work is free of errors of omission.

Acknowledgements

Huge thanks go to my patient and amazing graphics expert and cover designer, Carl Ulbrich of Jireh Communications. Great thanks and praise go to the key contributors, who touched my heart and kept my ring of fire ignited, with their generous and ingenious comments, photos, and lyrics. Endless gratitude goes to my husband, Ron Button, whose limitless humor, love, and encouragement keep my wings aloft.

Highest praise and gratitude for the conception and completion of this book goes to the Divine, whose inspiration has filled me, my research, my skills, and these pages, from the beginning.

Kebba Buckley Button
The LifeTools Lady[sm]

Published by:

LifeTools Press
UpBeat Living Media
Phoenix, Arizona
www.kebba.com

First Printing June 21, 2011
Second Printing June 30, 2011

ISBN   978-0-615-50151-2

CONTENTS

Behold: I make all things new.

—*Revelation 21:5*

Figure 1.   Shadow of Mont Ste. Michel, France. Photo by Carol Young

Chapter 1:
Personal Peace

My first book, **Discover The Secret Energized You**, addressed the ongoing exhaustion people have from a stress-accumulating lifestyle. It covered causes and solutions for stress. It offered that *people can actually trade in their stress* habits for energizing habits and end up feeling younger and more vital. In taking this material to groups, I was surprised to find most people don't have a calm center to touch in with. Most people don't have *peace within*. While my book offered ways to calm down, to feel more centered, and release stress, it did not cover creating and building up a personal inner reservoir of utterly serene centeredness. I have heard motivational speakers and pastors exhort people: "Don't let anyone steal your peace!" But what if a person has no fundamental inner peace? This book, then, is a tool for people to use in looking for that calm, sure center, or building it, or strengthening the *peace within* they do already have.

Do you believe that life is basically good? In 1963, in the United States of America, the national mood was relatively optimistic and peaceful. Then, in November, President John F. Kennedy was shot to death in Dallas, in front of many people. There was widespread shock and sadness. Individuals were jolted out of their sense of well-being. In schools, teachers went into the hallways and whispered to each other. Finally, the students were told why the teachers were whispering. There was astonishment, upset, and tears. Across the country, churches opened their sanctuaries for those who sought to process their pain, to find their *peace within* once more.

Now, almost 50 years later, life in the USA is mainly urban, busy, and noisy. People hold their cellphones and iPods close. Many live such a mental life and in such concentrated communication that they check and send email on a computer or phone while attending a live meeting. War, tsunamis, floods, fires, recessions, national security and budget issues, together with crowded populations, erode people's confidence that life is indeed good. People seek relief from worry, fear, overstimulation, and generalized stress. They seek comfort, calm, serenity, relaxation, inner peace and "letting go".

And well they should. The bodymind system craves what will help it. We know from medical studies that there are many benefits of managing stress through relaxation. The renowned Mayo Clinic lists some of these positive health changes as: slowing heart rate, lowering blood pressure, slowing breathing, increasing blood flow to major muscles, reducing muscle tension and chronic pain, improving concentration, reducing anger and frustration, and boosting confidence to handle problems. Clearly, relaxing feels better than stressing. A number of approaches can help a person to achieve a state of physical relaxation.

Relaxing the body is not the same as *peace within*, but it can help get you there. *Peace within* is something more, a soul peace, a calm knowingness, a fully heart-installed faith that God is there and all is truly well, whatever the appearance of things. So, what if your relaxation efforts were coupled with terrific internal surety and serenity? What if your heart, mind, and soul were on board with your relaxation quest? What is this state that people seek? This book has called it *peace within*. However, it goes by various names: *serenity, soul ease, contentment, personal peace, sweet relief, inner peace, tranquility, peace of mind, soul peace, a calm heart, certainty, centeredness, wellbeing, mental peace,* and *State of Grace.* Perhaps you have heard other expressions for it.

Such personal peace may come in *transport moments*, as when you are looking at a newborn baby, or driving past a hidden brook's footbridge in a wooded area. Riding in a car that comes into a sudden, beautiful view of a mountain scape, you may find your "breath taken away". More peace may come when hiking a beautiful trail, watching the sun set over the ocean, or taking in the sunrise over the Grand Canyon. Some like to read a novel that transports them to another place or time, or both. Avid readers say reading the right book can completely restore an anxious mood to one of well-being. Many have experienced an

Figure 2. Red cliffs of Sedona, Arizona. Photo by Kebba Buckley Button.

immediate mood shift from looking at a humorous or heartwarming picture or cartoon. So many enjoy this effect that the Internet ripples daily with numerous light-hearted and inspirational series of photos, cartoons, and witticisms with illustrations.

Occasionally, we see a person who is clearly in a state of transcendent personal peace, and we somehow get a transfer effect, feeling more peaceful ourselves. This happened to me years ago, on a stressful day of travel. On returning from an engineering conference, I was dashing through the Pittsburgh airport, feeling tense, tired, and overworked, when I was absolutely riveted by a person going by. She was a nun, wearing a traditional habit. She was walking peacefully through the terminal, wearing an etheric expression of utter happy calm. Her slight smile reminded me of the ageless magnetism of Michelangelo's Mona Lisa. I stopped completely. I had to stare as she passed. Her unreasonable peace and calm, in a noisy and busy environment, translated profoundly into my body, mind, and soul. I was changed by her. Now, years later, every time I think of that nun, my mind and body re-set, and I feel tension and stress leave me. I go directly to *peace within*.

Some place-related experiences can give us a profound shift into *peace within*. Perhaps 10 years ago, I was in a small town in Colorado for Christmas. Framed by a stunning view of the Rockies, many towering, majestic pine trees surrounded our historic hotel. Late Christmas Eve, fresh snow began to fall. Having much on my mind, I bundled up to go walk among the dancing flakes. Stepping out into the moonlight, I could feel the tension start to leave my muscles. I prayed for clarity and peace, and for any guidance I might need for the season and the upcoming year. I had not been out in the night air for more than ten minutes before my cares and worries of the last year began to seem completely insignificant. Soon, I couldn't even think what my issues had been. Now walking in an inch of new snow, I looked up through the white-laden tree branches and deeply inhaled the sweet winter air. I felt surrounded by and filled with the Peace That Passes All Understanding. I felt the Divine

Presence. I experienced a deeper level of *peace within* than I had felt in many years. I walked on. When I finally stepped back into the hotel, I realized I had been transformed. Years later, still, just recalling that walk vividly brings back the experience and the utter serenity.

Sometimes, a single image can take us directly to our inner peaceful core. Sometimes, a photo, an expression, a poem, or a song verse can help us shift from feeling stressed to feeling blessed and completely calm. Would you like to be experiencing more inner calm or serenity? What images, sounds, or experiences have you had that have taken you to greater calm? What phrases have meant much to you and inspired your heart? Why not make a commitment to yourself, now, to nurture your inner quiet each day?

When we have a deep core of *peace within*, we enjoy life more and get very different results from people and situations. A story with apparently mundane elements illustrates this crucial connection: a condo owner comes home one day to find 5 major shade trees missing from the common-area landscape in front of her unit. *This doesn't sound like a spiritual journey story, does it?* Now the unit not only looks bare, but its value is reduced and the interior will be more expensive to heat during the summer. The condo owner at first feels devastated. She discovers the condo board had decided to remove trees that might interfere with the sidewalks. What are the condo owner's options? The trees are already gone. *Here is a spiritual decision point.* She can hire a lawyer and sue for losses and restoration. She can go around complaining bitterly to the neighbors and all who will listen. She can organize a protest. *Can you feel the stress and fatigue building up, considering these yang options?*

How can she get what she really wants, which, she realizes, is a replacement tree in a strategic spot for shade? The condo owner prays for guidance and taps into her personal peace. Relaxed, at-ease, and centered, she goes to the next Board meeting to make her request. She pleasantly jokes to the Board about setting up a cappuccino stand outside her unit, with a couple of those cute little café tables and some of those Italian-espresso-brand umbrellas, for shade. She gets the Board members laughing, and they promptly approve a new tree, installing it just where she wants it days later. Today, four years later, the tree is taller than the condo, and it provides cooling shade for the condo and two parking spaces. Not only does the condo owner benefit from decreased cooling bills and increased beauty of her condo, but community members benefit from the shade. One apparently mundane and secular episode, handled from a core of *peace within*, led to Spirit-driven results that will yet increase with time.

The benefits of finding and growing your *peace within* are these: you enjoy it, you have more pleasant responses to stress, and you get better results from your health, people, Life, and the Universe. The more you cultivate your *peace within*, the more benefits you will reap. The more apparently secular and mundane moments you recognize as spiritual opportunities, the more you will practice and grow your peaceful inner core. ***Discover The Secret Energized You*** posed the question: "Life is an experiment: What tools will you use?" How much will you use this most forgotten LifeTool of *peace within*? Yes, it's up to you.

Figure 3. Garden Guardian Monk. Photo by Kebba Buckley Button.

Chapter 2:
The Science of Peace Within

In 1995, I had the extraordinary opportunity to attend a holistic medical conference and hear early reports of medical effects that are now considered well-known. One researcher was documenting the effects of stress on the heart and nervous system. His team had found that if a person holds an angry thought for five minutes, the parasympathetic nervous system is negatively impacted in eight factors for six hours. In other words, holding an angry thought hurts your physical health for much more than the time you hold that thought. And how many of us, when we feel very angry, choose to switch off those thoughts and feelings after only 5 minutes?

At that research facility, there was a staff person with an especially tense personality. In designing their experiments, the researchers used him as the perfect example of a stressed person. While setting up one experiment, after the stressed staffer was connected to the measuring equipment, a researcher handed the man a tame rabbit that was a pet within the facility. Immediately, all the man's stress measures dropped. This story raises the question: what else can instantly drop all your tension? I believe the answer is: *peace within.*

Today, there is a great deal of research on brain states and how we may get the most from our brain and lifestyle with applied brainwave techniques. There are 5 types of brain waves: alpha, beta, gamma, delta, and theta. Some audio and visual devices are now being marketed to generate, "synch up" or "entrain" the desired brain wave types, to meet different goals. This author recommends extreme caution in utilizing any such systems, until a solid research basis has been established. You only have one brain to use for this lifetime, and it is unique and precious.

Figure 4. Passion for playing guitar. Photo by Sandy Reay.

Meditation methods have been used for centuries with very positive results increasingly documented. Landmark medical studies on the benefits of Transcendental Meditation, for example, were published as early as the 1970's. Anyone who desires to increase their experience of different brain wave patterns would be wise to try device-free meditation methods first and stay informed as the brainwave research evolves.

We all know people who are not at peace. We call them "stressed" or "conflicted". The bodymind effects of stress and conflict are very well documented. When we are agitated, the brain tends to be in a high beta state. When we are very relaxed, we may be in an alpha state.

There is now a rising belief that we can only manifest what we desire in life when we are in the right brain state: relaxed, and in alpha. Some say the alpha waves are the connection between the mind and the Spirit. The link here is through the concept of the Law of Attraction. In the right, calm and relaxed brain state, you are more "in the Flow" and access connection to the energy frameworks around you. You are more open to the information and inspiration the Divine has for you. You are more likely to get what you want, from people and from circumstances. This phenomenon may be explained by the Unified Field Theory, from physics. We are all connected by energy fields.

To understand better the idea of the brain helping us to attract, think of athletes. People in sports are known to increase their success by practicing visualizing their scoring very specifically. A golfer may visualize the golf ball going into the cup in a single stroke, a "hole in one". In baseball, a batter may visualize hitting every pitch that comes his way, sending the ball far into the outfield. Wayne Gretzky, the famous hockey player, pictured the hockey puck going straight into the scoring zone, every time he struck it; his continuous high-scoring results are legendary.

Visualizing desired results is an accepted practice in sports, as well as in other fields. Perhaps this works by synching up the thoughts of a desired result with a "rehearsal" of the nervous system and muscles carrying out the needed movements for success. Ernest Holmes, the founder of Science of Mind, called this pre-visualizing "The Law of Mental Equivalents."

Now think again of the stressed-out staffer in the lab. In his daily hyped-up state, would he easily be able to visualize an athletic result? What about visualizing meeting a great woman to date, and himself being very confident, gracious, and successful with her? What about visualizing getting a promotion? What if the woman of his dreams walked up to him and said "hello"? Would he be more able to respond effectively to great opportunities while in his maximum stress state, or in a relaxed, centered, clear-minded state?

If you are feeling negative, you are more likely to hold negative pictures in your mind and attract those negative things. Your nervous system will literally adjust instantly to your thoughts, and you will give off a negative "vibration". People can *feel* if someone is happy and serene, or unhappy, conflicted and stressed. Like attracts like. What you focus on most is what you get the most of. So it is crucial to stop focusing on your stress, frustration, and lack, whether of energy, money, or relationships. It is vital to focus on what you do want—perhaps serenity, vitality, friends, a great marriage, cash prosperity, or certain professional achievements.

There is an expression, "negative people are attracted to negative people, so if they're drawn to you, examine your attitude". So what kind of people and circumstances do you want to attract? Happy, joyful, grateful, spiritual, harmonious, connective, and creative people? Satisfying and rewarding work? Plenty of quiet and leisure time? Then you literally need to adjust your brain function and nervous system to those vibrations. You need to develop a sweet, strong inner core of *peace within.*

This book uses many spirit-, heart-, mind- and body cues to help those who want to get and develop their *peace within.* This book is not a text book, but an evocative book. It is designed for people to contemplate and return to often, to ponder what evokes *peace within* for themselves. Readers can make notes on their thoughts and responses, then repeat successes and explore the subject some more. There is always more to learn and try. *Peace within* is not a moment or an arrival point. It is a path that becomes more beautiful and satisfying, the further you go along it. There is always more ahead on the path.

May you have much joy in your journey!

Often people attempt to live their lives backwards; they try to have more things, or more money, in order to do more of what they want, so they will be happier. The way it actually works is the reverse. You must first be who you really are, then do what you need to do, in order to have what you want.

—*Margaret Young*

Chapter 3:
The Importance of Peace Within

The Kingdom of Heaven is within you.

—Luke 17:21

The most potent and beneficent forces are the stillest.

—John Burroughs

All man's miseries derive from not being able to sit quietly in a room alone.

—Blaise Pascal

Neither wealth nor splendor, but tranquility and occupation, give happiness.

—*Thomas Jefferson*

Figure 5. Sailing in the Bahamas. Photo by Sandy Reay.

Tension is who you think you should be. Relaxation is who you are.

—*Chinese Proverb*

You cannot control circumstances, my dear sir; man proposes and God disposes!

—*The Count of Monte Cristo*

The mind is never right but when it is at peace within itself.

—*Seneca (Lucius Annaeus Seneca, Roman philosopher and statesman, 4 BC to 65 AD)*

Nothing can bring you peace but yourself; nothing, but the triumph of principles.

—*Ralph Waldo Emerson*

Inner peace can't be purchased or earned, only shared.

—*Rev. Cay Randall-May*

Growth is the willingness to let reality be new every moment.

—*Deepak Chopra*

Life isn't about waiting for the storm to pass. It's about learning to dance in the rain.

—*Unknown*

There are only two ways to live your life. One is as though nothing is a miracle. The other is as though everything is a miracle.

—*Albert Einstein*

Walk With God

When you ask God to walk with you,
You will often get what you want and
Always what you need.

But…

When you ask God if you can walk with
Him, never shall you want and always
Shall you have Peace.

—*John C. Jens*

At any moment, you have a choice, that either leads you closer to your spirit or further away from it.

—*Thich Nhat Hanh*

When we are unable to find tranquility within ourselves, it is useless to seek it elsewhere.

—*Francois de La Rochefoucauld*

I try to take one day at a time, but sometimes several days attack me at once.

—*Jennifer Yane*

So long as you worry about finding peace, you will not. Let go of your concern, care, and fretfulness, and peace will find you.

—Rev. Cay Randall-May

The Constitution only gives people the right to pursue happiness. You have to catch it yourself.

—*Benjamin Franklin*

Our duty, as men and women, is to proceed as if limits to our ability did not exist. We are collaborators in creation.

—*Teilhard de Chardin*

Figure 6. Sunrise in Maine. Photo by Carol Young.

I was thinking about how people seem to read the Bible a whole lot more as they get older; then it dawned on me, they're cramming for their final exam.

—*George Carlin*

Chapter 4:
Moving Into Peace Within

Peace I leave with you. My peace I give to you. Not as the world gives do I give to you. Do not let your hearts be troubled or afraid.

—John 14:27

And we know that God makes all things work together for good, for those who love Him…

—*Romans 8:28*

Throw your heart over the fence and the rest will follow.

—*Norman Vincent Peale*

It's easy to build up walls to protect yourself, but God has construction plans in mind.

—*Joyce Meyer*

Finally, beloved, whatever is true, whatever is honorable, whatever is just, whatever is pure, whatever is pleasing, whatever is commendable, if there is any excellence and if there is anything worthy of praise, think about these things. Keep on doing the things that you have learned and received and heard and seen in me, and the God of peace will be with you.

—*Phillipians 4:8-9*

Fear less, hope more; Whine less, breathe more; Talk less, say more; Hate less, love more; And all good things are yours

—*Swedish Proverb*

Peace is present right here and now, in ourselves and in everything we do and see. Every breath we take, every step we take, can be filled with peace, joy, and serenity. The question is whether or not we are in touch with it. We need only to be awake, alive in the present moment.

—*Thich Nhat Hanh*

Think of yourself as "Higher Powered". Know that you cannot be separate or separated from the Divine.

—*Rev. Kebba Buckley Button*

Be still and know that I am God.

—*Psalm 46:10*

See how nature—trees, grass, grow in silence; see the stars, the moon, and the sun, how they move in silence…We need silence to be able to touch souls.

—*Mother Theresa*

The experiences that give me the strongest feelings of peace are when I am outdoors in nature. Being in the midst of nature's beauty fills me with a powerful sense of God's presence that is deeply peaceful.

—*Joanne Deck*

Late at night we'd sit around that camp fire and sing
I'd climb into my bedroll, dream what daylight would bring.

—*Sandy Reay (Montana Memories © 1995)*

Figure 7. Streamscape near Canyon Lake, Arizona. Photo by Kebba Buckley Button.

I discovered in one relationship that if I had hate, revenge, anger, unforgiveness, or sadness in my heart, there was no room for peace, caring, joy, forgiveness, or love.

—*John C. Jens*

Trust yourself— create the kind of self that you will be happy to live with all your life.

—*Golda Meir*

When we apply the four key steps to healing: setting intention for the highest good; relaxing and clearing the mind; blending with peace in all our thoughts and actions; and attuning to unconditional love, then the *Creative Response* follows. Our most powerful creation is inner peace.

—Rev. Cay Randall-May

One of the five hindrances to end suffering is avoidance, so the way to peace is not avoiding but understanding: angst, chaos, and pain.

—*Rev. Marvin Brown*

Knowing is not enough, we must apply. Willing is not enough, we must do.

—*Bruce Lee*

He gives strength to the weary and increases the power of the weak.

—*Isaiah 40:29, NIV*

Personal peace is an inside job. You need to choose it.

—*Rev. Kebba Buckley Button*

It's not what you do once in a while; it's what you do day in and day out that makes the difference.

—*Jenny Craig*

Don't be afraid of the space between your dreams and reality. If you can dream it, you can make it so.

—*Belva Davis*

I rest in calm trust and rely on the Law of Spirit to bring good into my experience.

—*Ernest Holmes*

Figure 8. Beebop the Cat modelling perfect peace. Photo by Mandy Pratt.

Chapter 5:
Choosing Peace Within

God always takes the simplest way.

—*Albert Einstein*

People usually consider walking on water or in thin air a miracle. But I think the real miracle is not to walk either on water or in thin air, but to walk on earth. Every day we are engaged in a miracle which we don't even recognize: a blue sky, white clouds, green leaves, the black, curious eyes of a child -- our own two eyes. All is a miracle.

—*Thich Nhat Hanh*

Before God we are all equally wise - and equally foolish.

—*Albert Einstein*

State Sues Over Assets of Defunct Peace Museum

Outside the air is filled with hail.
Winter's fury lingers. Once more
I put on mitts, wool coat and hat: my armor
- continue my quarrel with winter, a challenge
of late, my metabolism not what it used to be. Winter keeps me
off guard. Its notion: to wear me down. Ice covered
sidewalks freeze, thaw: predictable weapons of war
employed yearly like the changing of tires. Its hope:
catch me with the wrong footwear. A sudden squall: inevitable.

I wonder about its' plan to make me surrender. Stay indoors.
Cede territory. Peace,
something you could once read about
in a Chicago museum, impractical
as a John Lennon song or the guitar
he composed love on, an artifact
from the peace movement era,
so you can just imagine
how old man winter laughs at my ideas of peace,
proposals for a thaw in relations: this cold war.
Lately I've been trying to make peace
an organizing principle in my daily life.
I've used diplomatic channels, given winter notice
that I see snow removal as a last resort,
something not inevitable.
I refrain from making war.
I fall in love with the snow,

taste flakes on my tongue,
make snowmen, angels,
trails that zigzag: huge labyrinths
timeless pleasures wide as a smile.
I've been told my efforts are, technically speaking, impractical.
And yet, walking through this wonderland,
surrounding me like a warm blanket,
is this bliss.

—Ray McGinnis

Figure 9. Ice-coated weeds, Colorado. Photo by Sandy Reay.

Figure 10. Portland Head Light Lighthouse, Maine. Photo by Carol Young.

When we are mindful, deeply in touch with the present
moment, our understanding of what is going on
deepens, and we begin to be filled with acceptance, joy,
peace and love.

— *Thich Nhat Hanh*

To no peculiar lot in life
is happiness confined,
but to the self-approving heart
and firm, contented mind.

—*Unknown*

You can say I'm a dreamer and a drifter
You can say that my pathways are my own
You can say that I go just where the wind blows
Before the leaves turn golden, I find I'm headin' home.

—Sandy Reay and B.J. Suter (Lady of the Valley © 1996)

Inner peace is innate in humans. Everyone has the capacity to experience the end of suffering, which is peace. That is the third of the Four Noble Truths taught by Buddha and foundation of Buddhism: "There is an end to suffering." How to access it? I think that we look for the things that allow us to see peace and hold them in our focus. It is like a glass filled with dirty allowed to sit. Eventually the dirt will fall to the bottom and one can see through the glass clearly. Once our emotions have settled we are able to look at the angst, chaos, and pain and not be attached to the sensations.

—Rev. Marvin Brown

Say to yourself, over and over:
"Walk in peace, stay in Love."

—Joyce Meyer Ministries conference staff (advice to volunteers for dealing with difficult people and situations)

May today there be peace within. May you trust that you are exactly where you are meant to be. May you not forget the infinite possibilities that are born of faith in yourself and others. May you use the gifts that you have received, and pass on the love that has been given to you. May you be content with yourself just the way you are. Let this knowledge settle into your bones, and allow your soul the freedom to sing, dance, praise and love. It is there for each and every one of us.

—St. Therese of Lisieux

Breathing in, I calm body and mind. Breathing out, I smile. Dwelling in the present moment I know this is the only moment.

—Thich Nhat Hanh

Got the boot... again. I'm oddly at peace with it, though. :) When a door gets slammed, God opens an apartment complex clubhouse.

—Emi Bauer

Many people think excitement is happiness.... But when you are excited you are not peaceful. True happiness is based on peace.

—Thich Nhat Hanh

Heaven lies about us, not only in our infancy, but all our lives.

—Hugh Black

Joy is the Grace we say to God.

—Jean Ingelow

The mind can go in a thousand directions, but on this beautiful path, I walk in peace. With each step, the wind blows. With each step, a flower blooms.

—Thich Nhat Hanh

Chapter 6:
Touched by Grace/Holy Spirit

It's the overwhelming awe, joy and beauty of the Universe and the deep sense of connectedness to the World that we all seek.

—*Albert Einstein*

And that peace which comes from the innermost recesses of the Spirit is left with us: a peace which the world cannot take away, for it springs from the bosom of the Father of light, love, life and wisdom.

—*Ernest Holmes*

Divine love is always at work for every man, whether he knows it or not.

—*Unknown*

Inner peace is a State of Grace: a baby having just been fed, diaper changed, resting on their mother's chest and surrounded by that familiar heartbeat. Inner peace is right here, right now, just a decision away. We always have the capacity to experience joy and peace in every moment if that is what we choose to see.

—*Rev. Marvin Brown*

Never lose an opportunity of seeing anything that is beautiful; for beauty is God's handwriting—a wayside sacrament.

—*Ralph Waldo Emerson*

Figure 11. Roses, The Portland Rose Garden. Photo by Carol Young.

I'm an April desert morning. I'm a flower fresh with dew.

—Sandy Reay (Sandstorm From Sedona ©2006)

When God takes something from your grasp, He's not punishing you, but merely opening your hands to receive something better.

—*Unknown*

The will of God will never take you where the Grace of God will not protect you.

—*Unknown*

Or in the night, imagining some fear,
How easily is a bush supposed a bear?
—*William Shakespeare,*
A Midsummer Night's Dream Act 1 Scene 5
Theseus speaking

But in the morning's golden rays
Sits a fiery dragon with icy gaze

Yet with God's love and Grace
The Holy Spirit is my brace.

—*John C. Jens*

God is in all, over all, and through all.

—*Ernest Holmes*

In all chaos there is a Cosmos, in all disorder a secret Order.

—*Carl Jung*

I ask God from the wealth of His glory to give you power through His Spirit to be strong in your inner selves, and I pray that Christ will make His home in your hearts through faith. I pray that you may have your roots and foundation in love, so that you, together with all God's people, may have the power to understand how broad and long, how high and how deep, is Christ's love. Yes, may you come to know His love -- although it can never be fully known -- and so be completely filled with the very nature of God.

—*Ephesians 3:16-19*

The strength of a man consists in finding out the way God is going, and going that way.

—*Henry Ward Beecher*

Oh, the limitless horizon is not big enough to hold
All the love I feel within me, or the peace that's in my soul.

—Sandy Reay (Road Song ©1994)

Let our never-ceasing care be to better the love that we offer our fellows. One cup of this love that is drawn from the Spring on the mountain is worth a hundred taken from the stagnant well of ordinary charity.

—Maurice Maeterlinck

Do the best you can where you are and, when that is accomplished, God will open a door for you, and a voice will call, "Come up hither into a higher sphere."

—Henry Ward Beecher

There's a Divinity that shapes our ends,
Rough-hew them how we will.

—William Shakespeare

The Visitors

Sometimes you look at a black pond
like this and the water is filled
with stars. And ancient apple trees,
gnarled branches in search of
something. Out of the woods three fauns
with their mother stare at you 'cross
meadows, motionless as the trees,
then lower their heads to nibble
a long time. And something as
imperceptible as stardust
fills you, whispers *yes*, then passes.
The deer gone. The meadow empty.

—Ray McGinnis

Figure 12. Deer feeding at Parker, Colorado. Photo by Sandy Reay.

Chapter 7:
God is Everywhere

Coincidence is God's way of remaining anonymous.
—*Albert Einstein*

Vocatus atque non vocatus, Deus aderit.
(Bidden or unbidden, God is present.)

—*Desiderius Erasmus quoting a Spartan proverb* (popularized by
Swiss psychiatrist Carl Jung, who had it inscribed over his home's doorway
and also on his tombstone)

Make yourself familiar with the angels, and behold them
frequently in spirit; for without being seen, they are present with
you.

—*St. Francis de Sales*

Surely the Lord is in this place, and I was unaware of it! …This
is none other than the house of God: this is the gate of Heaven.

—*Genesis 28:16-17*

Wherever you are, you are standing on holy ground.

—*Rev. Kebba Buckley Button*

There is no spot
 where God is not.

—*Ron Button*

And we will waltz with the moon
And play hide 'n' seek with the stars
Till the morning runs with the rising sun
And nobody knows where we are.

—*Sandy Reay and B.J. Suter (Car Full of Collies © 2008)*

His truth endures to all generations.

—Psalm 100:5

Figure 13. Chihuly glass boulders at the Desert Botanical Garden, Phoenix.
Photo by Kebba Buckley Button.

Chapter 8:
When You Are Troubled

Don't panic—this is only a test.

—Joyce Meyer

Never think that God's delays are God's denials. Hold on; hold fast; hold out. Patience is genius.

—Comte de Buffon

If something we have always had is giving out, it only means that something better is ready to take its place.

—Christian Science Sentinel

And I said to the man who stood at the gate of the year: "Give me a light that I may tread safely into the unknown." And he replied: "Go out into the darkness and put your hand into the Hand of God. That shall be to you better than light and safer than a known way."
So I went forth, and finding the Hand of God, trod gladly into the night. And He led me towards the hills and the breaking of day in the lone East."

—*Minnie Louise Haskins(British writer and lecturer at the London School of Economics), 1908, from the poem, "God Knows"*

There is no education like adversity.

—*Benjamin Disraeli*

I can do all things through Christ who strengthens me.

—*Phillipians 4:13*

Say, "So I'm up for anything!"

—*Rev. Kebba Buckley Button*

I am not discouraged, because every wrong attempt discarded is another step forward.

—*Thomas A. Edison*

I cannot give you a formula for success, but I can give you the formula for failure – which is: try to please everybody.

—*Herbert Bayard Swope*

Please God first. Who is in charge, anyway?

—*Rev. Kebba Buckley Button*

Let go and let God.

—Unknown

Experience is one thing you can't get for nothing.

—*Oscar Wilde*

Feeling troubled? Just pray. The main thing is to relax and let the Lord carry you.

—*Patricia DePottey*

No one can steal your peace. You have to hand it off to them.

—*Rev. Kebba Buckley Button*

All things change, but God remains!

—*Mary Arnold Ward*

Nil illegitimi carborundum.
(Pseudo Latin: Don't let the bastards wear you down.)

—*Unknown*

Fond as we are of our loved ones, there comes at times, during their absence, an unexplainable peace.

—*Anne Shaw*

Deal with the faults of others as gently as with your own.
—*Chinese proverb*

Write the bad things that are done to you in sand, but write the good things that happen to you on a piece of marble.

—*Arabic Proverb*

One of the secrets of a long and happy life is to forgive everybody everything before you go to sleep each night.

—*Bernard Baruch*

Trust doesn't always require an answer.

—*Joyce Meyer*

When I realize that I am not feeling peaceful, perhaps when I'm driving, I become aware that I have forgotten momentarily how much God loves me. I become conscious of my breathing and slowly repeat to myself, "God loves me" until I feel peace settle in again. Then, I find that I've put into perspective the situation that was troubling me, and now I recognize that all really is well. Any guidance I need comes to me when I do this. Very effective!

—*Joanne Deck*

You have to go through the test to get to the testimony. Some people only get the "moanies".

—*Joyce Meyer*

Tomorrow is a new day; begin it well and serenely, and with too high a spirit to be cumbered with your old nonsense.

—*Ralph Waldo Emerson*

If we are peaceful, if we are happy, we can smile and blossom like a flower, and everyone in our family, our entire society, will benefit from our peace.

—*Thich Nhat Hanh*

He who laughs, lasts!

—*Mary Pettibone Poole*

It is well with my soul.

—*Horatio Spafford (From a poem of the same name, later made into lyrics for a hymn of the same name. Spafford was a happy, successful, wealthy married attorney, who lost a son, many of his holdings, and then all four daughters, in a several year span. A devout Christian, he wrote the poem in1873, on a sea voyage to reunite with his wife, after the daughters drowned. The poem expresses faith that no matter what happens, in faith, you can choose to say "it is well with my soul".*

When life's circumstances and troubles are at their worst, peace within can nonetheless be strongest if we apply the four key steps to healing: setting intention for the highest good; relaxing and clearing the mind; blending with peace in all our thoughts and actions; and attuning to unconditional love.

—*Rev. Cay Randall-May*

From time to time, to remind ourselves to relax and be peaceful, we may wish to set aside some time for a retreat, a day of mindfulness, when we can walk slowly, smile, drink tea with a friend, enjoy being together as if we are the happiest people on Earth.

—*Thich Nhat Hanh*

Do not be anxious about anything. But in everything by prayer and supplication, with thanksgiving, let your requests be made known unto God. And the peace of God, which surpasses all understanding, shall guard your hearts and minds through Christ Jesus.

—Philippians 4:6-7

Others can stop you temporarily -- you are the only one who can do it permanently.

—Zig Ziglar

Whatever you can do, or dream you can, begin it. Boldness has genius, power, and magic in it.

—Goethe

Don't give up—Moses was once a basket case.

—Sign at the Eastside Baptist Church, Phoenix, Arizona

And the peace of God that passes all understanding will keep your hearts and minds in Christ Jesus.

—Phillipians 4:7

May the Lord bless you and keep you,
May the Lord make his face shine upon you
And be gracious unto you.
May the Lord lift up His countenance upon you
And give you peace.

—Priestly blessings, Numbers 6:24-26

Key Contributors

Emi Bauer is a web designer for small- and home-based businesses. A longtime Toastmaster, she loves learning about different communication and leadership styles. This is especially helpful for her as a wife and the mother of 3 ADHD boys. As webmaster for the Phoenix Chapter of Women of Visionary Influence (WOVI Inc.), she is known for her cheerful laugh and her love of the mentoring program. Emi chooses the most positive options and the humor in any situation. Learn more about Emi's work at www.eBauerWebServices.com .

Rev. Marvin Brown is uniquely qualified to blend together Eastern philosophy with Western thought. Starting out in his family's newspaper business as a writer/reporter and working many years in the printing industry, he understands the challenges of being deadline driven and being enmeshed in the stress of the corporate world.

Rev. Marvin is ordained in the Order of Interbeing (Tiep Hien), founded by Ven. Thich Nhat Hanh, a Buddhist Order. He is also an ordained non-denominational minister through the International Council of Community Churches and a New

Thought minister through the Community Church of New Thought. Marvin's friends often refer to him as a displaced monk. His students report that his clear, simple, and diverse way of explaining things makes mindfulness easy to understand and apply. Marvin leads an internet community practice, Mindfulness Anywhere. Learn more about Marvin at: www.mindfulnessanywhere.com . Follow him on Twitter: @MarvinBrown, or FaceBook: @MindfulMarvin .

Joanne Musson Deck is a certified wellness consultant and lifestyle coach. She has over 20 years of experience helping people adopt healthy habits that enable them to look, feel, and be their very best. She is the author of the award winning guide to dating in the new millennium, *Sane Sex for Singles*. Joanne is a regular speaker for corporations, singles groups, churches, and civic organizations. To learn more about her speaking, training, and coaching and her latest book, *Learning to Receive with Grace and Ease*, visit www.joannedeck.com.

Nancy Harper, AIA, is a registered architect who enjoys photography. She has designed, planned and managed building projects in seven states. She is a member of the American Institute of Architects, The Frank Lloyd Wright Foundation, the New Vision Center, and the Desert Botanical Garden.

Nancy holds the *Master of Architecture* degree from the University of New Mexico, and the *Bachelor of Architecture* degree from the University of Southern California, Los Angeles. In addition to buildings, landscape and art, include the history of the United States, spiritual writings, and Hindu meditation/chanting. Reach her at: **naharper.arch@gmail.com**

and see her sample projects at:
http://www.slideshare.net/troy32659 .

John C. Jens, *imago dei*, is a spiritual being on a human journey experiencing God's grace and beauty of creation. His wonderful wife, Sara, is also experiencing her own journey; they often share experiences, such as two granddaughters. From a former marriage he has three adult sons who are all productive members of society. Contributing to John's understanding are life experiences as a life-long-Lutheran, a Stephen Ministry Leader, a retired Army officer and master instructor, an active member of many professional and spiritual communities. John is a certified professional geologist with the US Army Corps of Engineers and an adjunct professor at a local community college. And, he is a sometimes poet when God gives him something to write.

Ray McGinnis is the author of *Writing the Sacred: A Psalm-inspired Path to Appreciating and Writing Sacred Poetry*. A member of the Advisory Board of the Institute for Poetic Medicine, in Mountain View, CA, Ray has taught over 10,000 people in journal writing and in poetry workshops across North America. A member of The Writer's Union of Canada, Ray lives in Vancouver, Canada. For more information about his background visit his website: www.writetotheheart.com .

Mandy Pratt is the author of 2 self help books. She has conducted over 12,000 hours of one on one coaching with clients from all around the world. Her passion is training and helping other people to become coaches. Her photo of Beebop The Cat, modeling *peace within*, was taken in a sunny moment of 2011. You can find out more about Mandy: www.MandyPratt.com .

Rev. Cay Randall-May, Ph.D. is the author of *Healing and the Creative Response. Four Key Steps Shared by Healers and Artists* (CayMay Press with Brooks Goldmann Publishing, 2010), Rev. Randall-May has worked as a professional intuitive consultant, medical intuitive, and healer for more than 30 years. Among her passions are her husband and family, teaching intuitive skills to others, writing, painting, and gardening. To learn more about her readings, classes, and appearances including radio shows, please visit: www.HealingCreativeResponse.com; www.cayrandallmay.com; www.cayrandallmaysart.com; befriend her on Facebook; or email crandallmayphx@aol.com.

Sandy Reay is a musician, songwriter and photographer. In 2010, she published *I Wanted to Fly*, a CD of her original and co-written songs. Several songs have gotten airplay, and been recorded by other musicians. One was a Western Music Association 2010 Finalist for Best Original Song. She also taught computer science, bred collies, run rivers in a rubber raft, built computer software systems, lived on a horse ranch, worked on a drill rig, and was the first woman gas station attendant in Colorado. She still hasn't decided what she wants to be when she grows up. For more information about Sandy's music, please go to www.ColoradoSandstormMusic.com.

Carol Young is a retired woman who wants to look back on life and feel she's done a little good but had a lot of fun. She was a therapist who worked with the mentally ill and now works as a volunteer special advocate for kids in the foster care system.

Carol was in the stadium when the Diamondbacks won the World Series. She's seen London, Paris & Spain. She has 3 cats, the favorite of which she rescued from her garage 9 years ago. She got to see the live launch of a space shuttle. Carol's proudest accomplishment was taking up the piano at age 63, satisfying a lifelong desire. And it never fails to amaze her that circles on lines can produce a beautiful melody.

Carol uses humor to maintain sanity when things go a little haywire. She likes indie movies, music, her Color Nook, and goes to the theater when she can. She has "glass half full" view of the world. Oh and she loves to take and share photos!

About the Author

She is an ordained minister and former engineering manager, and an award-winning author and speaker. Rev. Kebba Buckley Button wants you to live the life you've always wanted. Every day can be new, with all your options open. How about some fresh outlooks and strategies for your body, mind, and spirit? Would you like to learn to call in the life qualities you yearn for?

Rev. Kebba's award-winning book, *Discover The Secret Energized You,* reveals the stress-welcoming strategies that most people are using, that they don't even realize they are using. It then offers easy, fun new approaches, to get the energy, wellness, joy, and relationships you've been seeking. Rev. Kebba's meditation CD, *Receptive and Ready,* is designed for people who want change and don't know why it isn't happening. This CD moves people forward, from an energy level, as well as from strategy. Life is to be enjoyed! The new book, *Peace Within,* assists people in finding and enriching their peaceful inner core.

As a corporate stress management trainer, Kebba has presented many programs for such diverse groups as: CableOne; the Presbytery of Grand Canyon; Unity of Phoenix; the law firm of Brobeck, Pfleger, and Harrison; the American Association of Public Welfare Attorneys, and many church, business and social organizations. She has appeared on KPNX TV (NBC), as well as KNXV-TV (ABC). For more information on Kebba, her links, programs and products: www.kebba.com .